WE BOTH READ®

Introduction

We Both Read books are perfect to read with a buddy—or to read by yourself! If you are reading the book alone, you can read it like any other book. If you are reading with another person, you can take turns reading aloud. When taking turns, it's a good idea for the reader with more experience to read the more difficult parts, marked with a red star ✪ or a red splash ✳. The reader with less experience can read the parts marked with a blue star ✪ or a blue splash ✳.

Sharing the reading of a book can be a lot of fun, and reading aloud is a great way to improve fluency and expression. If you are reading with someone else, you might also want to take the time to talk about what you are reading and what else you know or would like to learn about horses! After reading with someone else, you might even want to experience reading the entire book on your own.

We Both Read: The Horse Lover's Book

Published under license from Editions Milan/Groupe Bayard
Copyright © 2004 Editions Milan –
300, rue Léon Joulin – 31101 Toulouse Cedex 9 – France

Written by Stéphanie Ledu
Illustrated by Cécile Hudrisier

Photography by Bios (Klein/Hubert, Klein, Nicolotti Muriel, Gunther Michel), Blue Box
(Ronald Wittek, Manuel Behrendt, Harscher Reiner, Harald Luder, Liedtke Benrnd),
Bridgeman-Giraudon, Cheval D'Aventure/Anne Mariage, Cogis (Labat, Monnier, Miriski,
Delaborde, Gissey, Hermeline, Vidal, Varin), Colibri (L. Chaix, J. Delpech, F. et J.-L. Ziegler,
J.-A. Mayet, L. Chocat, Magnin, J. Joannet, P. Fontaine, D. Alet, R. Toulouse, C. Baranger,
J.-Y. Lavergne), Gilles Delaborde, Hoa-Qui (Age), Optipress (Sabine Stuewer, Bob Langrish,
Ardina Struwer, Annette Soumillard, Alain Laurioux, Anne-Sophie Flament, Frédéric Chéhu,
Florence Toubon), Phone (Grenet/Soumillar, Valter Raymond, Ferrero/Labat),
Photo12.com/Collection Cinema and Milan/P. Massacret

The envelope activity on p. 49 is provided courtesy of Cheval Magazine and Cheval Star

English Translation Copyright © 2008 by Treasure Bay, Inc.
Translated by Wendy Helfenbaum/Take Two Productions
English Edition Edited by Sindy McKay

Published by Treasure Bay, Inc.
40 Sir Francis Drake Boulevard
San Anselmo, CA 94960 USA

PRINTED IN SINGAPORE

Library of Congress Catalog Card Number: 2007907990

Hardcover ISBN-10: 1-60115-019-9
Hardcover ISBN-13: 978-1-60115-019-6
Paperback ISBN-10: 1-60115-020-2
Paperback ISBN-13: 978-1-60115-020-2

We Both Read® Books
Patent No. 5,957,693

Visit us online at: **www.webothread.com**

WE BOTH READ®

The Horse Lover's Book

By Stéphanie Ledu

Illustrated by Cécile Hudrisier

Table of Contents

TREASURE BAY

★ Hello! My name is Lily!

Do you love horses like I do?
Then you've come to the right place to
share your passion. Together we'll learn
how to take care of them, how to ride them,
and how to better understand them.
Come with me and let's enter
the kingdom of the horse!

3 ☆ IT'S "HIPP" TO LOVE HORSES!

☆ THE GREEK WORD FOR HORSE IS "HIPPOS." THAT'S WHY THE STUDY OF HORSES IS CALLED "HIPPOLOGY." IF YOU LOVE STUDYING HORSES, YOU'RE A HIPPOLOGIST!

BLAZE

WHORL

STOCKING

✪ WHAT MAKES ME SPECIAL?

Most horses have some kind of special markings that set them apart from others.

☀ A "blaze" is a wide stripe down the middle of the face.

☀ A "snip" is a white spot on the nose.

☀ "whorls" are fur that grows in all directions.

☀ "Stockings" are leg markings that go up to my knees.

✪ Name That Body Part

A horse has legs, ears, and a mouth—just like we do. But some parts of his body have special names, like "flank" and "hoof" and "hock." Every good hippologist needs to know these names.

BEAUTY TIPS

You love me—so you think I'm beautiful! But there are other factors that determine my level of quality. I must fulfill the standards of my breed and be properly built to do the job I was bred for.

BLACK   BAY   BUCKSKIN   GRAY   CHESTNUT

✪ What color is my coat?

The hair on a horse's body is called its "coat." The color of a horse's coat falls into four main classifications. It sounds simple enough, but it can be kind of tricky . . .

☆ 1 ALL BLACK!

Its coat and mane are made up of only black hairs. Easy . . . but not very common!

BLACK

BUCKSKIN

BAY

2 BLACK AND OTHER

This is the family of horses with black manes and black lower legs. Their coat might be:

red,
a "bay",
yellow,
a buckskin,
gray,
a "gray".

GRAY

HAUNCH
TAIL
CROUP
LOINS
BACK
WITHERS
POLL
MANE
EAR
FORELOCK
FOREHEAD
CHEEK
NOSTRIL
MOUTH
SHOULDER
CHEST
FOREARM
KNEE
CANNON
PASTERN
CORONET
HAUNCH
QUARTER
STOMACH
FLANK
GIRTH
HOCK
STIFLE
CHESTNUT
ANKLE
HOOF
FETLOCK
REAR LEGS
FRONT LEGS

PALOMINO

PINTO

3
NO BLACK MANE
These are "chestnut" horses. They have names based on their color:

Red with a red mane : a "chestnut"

Yellow with a tan mane : a "palomino"

CHESTNUT

4
OTHER FAMILIES
These horses are identified by the markings on their coats. For example, pinto horses have large white markings all over their body.

PALOMINO

PINTO

♥ ♥ SEEING SPOTS! ♥ ♥

THE APPALOOSA
In the 18th century, at the edge of the Palouse river in northeastern United States, the Nez Perce Indians bred horses with beautiful spotted coats. Each coat was different, making it easier to tell them apart!

LET'S TALK ABOUT HORSE SENSE

⭐ A HORSE'S SENSES ARE MUCH MORE DEVELOPED THAN OURS. WHY? BECAUSE IN THE WILD, A HORSE IS EASY PREY AND MUST COUNT ON HIS EYES, EARS, AND NOSE TO SENSE APPROACHING DANGER!

⭐ I see you!

We horses have a wide field of vision. We can see the grass we're grazing on and the fence in the distance — all at the same time. But we can't see four feet in front of our face! We have a blind spot there, so please approach us from the side instead.

⭐ I HAVE STRONG EARS

When you want to pinpoint a sound, you turn your whole head. Not me! With sixteen muscles each, my ears can turn in all directions — all by themselves. My ears can hear ultrasonic (very high-pitched) and infrasonic (very low) tones while you hear. . .only silence.

⭐ I have big eyes

You have eyes on the front of your head. I have one on each side. This allows me to see all around — except right in front and right behind me. I can even see you when you're up on my back. So please don't make any sudden moves up there: it gives me quite a scare!

⭐ BINOCULAR VISION

MONOCULAR VISION (LEFT EYE)

MONOCULAR VISION (RIGHT EYE)

BLIND SPOT

✪ BOY DO I SMELL!

I live in a world of smells that you know nothing about... For example, I can smell your fear by the odor of your sweat! With my nose in the wind, I can sniff out an enemy, find food, and even locate water from many miles away.

✪ I HAVE GOOD TASTE...

First, I sniff—then I eat. My nose can tell me if a plant is tasty or toxic! Like you, I can distinguish between four flavors: bitter, acidic, salty, and sweet. I have a preference for the last one. How about you?

✪ YUCK!

MOST OF US HORSES DON'T LIKE THE SMELL OF PERFUME. OR CIGARETTES!

✪ A NOSE-Y HANDSHAKE

EXPERT ADVICE

To get to know one another, two horses will sniff each other for a long time. Each will remember the odor of the other for the rest of his life! Your horse recognizes you this way as well: to say hello, blow softly into his nostrils.

WHAT DID YOU SAY?

⭐**WHAT DO YOU WANT?**

Ears laid back and teeth showing: do not approach. I'm mad!

⭐MANY TIMES PEOPLE CAN TELL WHAT KIND OF MOOD YOU ARE IN JUST BY LOOKING AT YOU. IT IS THE SAME WAY WITH HORSES! JUST WATCH CLOSELY...

⭐Talking with his ears

NOTHING TO REPORT

Ears still and relaxed: calm and content.

⭐**GULP! HELP ME!**

Ears pointed backwards, muscles tensed: fearful.

⭐**HEY! WHAT IS THAT?**

Ears pointed forward: paying attention.

⭐**I'M NOT SURE I LIKE THAT...**

Ears towards the front, moving in all directions: anxious.

Talking with his body

✪ WATCH OUT!

Irritated, the tail swings in the air. Then the back end turns toward the intruder to intimidate him. Whoa! Here comes a kick!

✪ DO NOT DISTURB

Eyelids are closed, head is down, and lip hangs down... Sssh... it's time for a snooze. A horse sleeps "standing up" about three hours a day.

✪ Do you speak "horse"?

Can a horse really talk? Well, not with words like you and I do. But he does make seven basic sounds—and they all mean something different!

✪ WELL, WHAT ARE WE WAITING FOR?

Pawing the ground, scratching the soil with his hoof: this horse is worried... or he is simply hungry and wants his fair share of food!

✪ ISN'T LIFE GREAT!

A horse rolls on the ground, gets up and takes off at a gallop. Don't worry—he's just having a little fun! It's a good sign that he's in excellent health.

✪ ● The NEIGH : when two horses leave or greet each other...You can hear it over a half mile away!

● A soundless SHUDDER : often used by a female (mare) calling her baby (foal.)

● The GRUNT : a very loud snort out the nose that shows worry or fear.

✪ ● The EXHALE : whew! The horse sneezes to clear dust or insects out of his nose.

● The SIGH : a gentle shudder, sent out by two close friends

● The SQUEAL : a brief, sharp sound that says "Watch out!" or "Leave me alone!"

✪ ● The GROWL : A sound that is quite low, signaling discomfort or fatigue.

HAPPY BIRTHDAY!

I JUST GOT HERE! HERE ARE SOME PICTURES THAT TELL THE STORY OF MY BIRTH...

NAME : Poppy

BIRTH DATE : May 10

WEIGHT : 110 pounds

⭐ MY FATHER

The breeder chose him because he is beautiful and has a good personality. I will never meet him. But I will certainly inherit some of his qualities!

⭐ MY MOTHER

She carried me for 11 months, but you could only notice her big belly during the last four months. She stopped working at that time, and was very well taken care of.

⭐ HELLO, WORLD!

When my mother sensed that I was about to be born, she lay down on her side. Her amniotic sac broke. My legs, then my head appeared. In just a few minutes, I had arrived!

My Birth

GROOMING

Mommy licked me to clean me up and keep me warm. This also helped us to learn each others' scent.

ALREADY ON MY FEET

A half-hour after my birth, I was already standing. My legs were still a little shaky, though.

FIRST FEEDING

Being born is hard work. I was really hungry! I'm always hungry. The first month of my life, I nursed about 70 times a day!

⭐ I'm growing up!

⭐ MY FIRST OUTING

Oh! Look at the beautiful butterfly! I trot behind him . . . my mom grunts to call me back to her. Earlier today, I tried to taste some toxic plants . . . and mom growled for me to leave them alone. I always listen to my mom!

⭐ WHAT IS IMPRINTING?

It means getting a young colt used to being around humans as soon as he's born. The breeder lies him down and holds him still so that he will be tame later on. He slides his hand inside the colt's mouth to symbolize the bit and taps on his feet to get him used to being worked on by a blacksmith in the future . . . It takes a real professional to do this job!

⭐ MY GAMES

I love to play racing games with my friends. Sometimes we like to pretend to fight. We rear up and "box" with our front legs!

⭐ 💜 A BREED FOR SPEED 💜

THE ENGLISH THOROUGHBRED

In the 18th century, English breeders imported three stallions from the Orient to breed with their fastest mares. The result: some very, very fast foals! And so the English thoroughbred race horse was born. Today, their descendants can gallop almost 40 miles per hour at race-tracks around the world.

⭐ COME CLOSE, DON'T BE AFRAID!

IF YOU APPROACH A HORSE CORRECTLY, HE WILL FEEL CONFIDENT WITH YOU. AND YOU WILL FEEL CONFIDENT, TOO!

⭐ Here I come!

If your horse is in the field, stay behind the fence and call to him. Make sure he sees you! Now enter and walk to him, with halter in hand. Keep talking to him.

When you reach your horse, hold out your hand so that he can sniff it and pet his neck. Now put on his halter.

⭐ IT'S EASY!

1 Place yourself to the left of your horse, near his head. Hold the halter by the top of its sidepiece, and slip on the noseband by raising it up to the middle of his face.

2 With your right hand, gently place the crown piece behind his ears.

3 Buckle the halter on the left side.

⭐ And we're off!

Hold the rope with your right hand next to the halter and your left hand at the end. If the rope is too long, fold it over. Never roll the rope around your hand! If your horse pulled away quickly, you could be hurt. Place yourself to the left of your horse, a little bit in front of his shoulder. Walk at the same pace as him… and watch where you're going!

⭐ Code of Conduct

▲ Rule number 1: Never approach a horse from the back, unless you want to be kicked!

▲ Rule number 2: Even if you are very happy to see him, do not run or yell—and no sudden movements.

▲ Rule number 3: If you are angry or upset, calm down before approaching.

⭐ THE HALTER

NOSEBAND   SIDEPIECE

CROWN PIECE

LEAD ROPE

RING TO ATTACH THE LEAD ROPE

⭐ THE RIGHT KNOT

Learn the right way to tie up your horse. The "quick release knot" is easy to untie with just one hand.

TIE RING

STRING

LOOP

LOOP

FOLD

FOLDED END   FREE END

1 Pass the rope through the tie ring. Bring it over onto itself by making a loop.

2 Refold the free end of the rope. Pass it behind the end that is holding the horse, then through the loop.

3 Pull on the folded end. To undo the knot, pull on the free end.

EXPERT ADVICE

⭐ This book contains a lot of useful information about horses. However, before you try anything you haven't done before, it's always important to talk about it with your parents and get instructions from adults who know about horses and riding. Always make sure you have adults around when you are with horses, particularly when you are trying anything new. This is for your safety and the safety of the horses.

A GROOMING EXPERT

HORSES SWEAT AND GET DIRTY, JUST LIKE YOU! A GOOD GROOMING MAKES HIM LOOK—AND FEEL—SO MUCH BETTER.

2 To remove the dirt loosened by the curry comb, brush with the brush: first against the direction of the hair, then in the direction of the hair.

BRUSH

1 The curry comb loosens dirt and dead hair. Brush with it in a circular motion, avoiding your horse's head and his joints.

CURRY COMB

☆ Thank you!

When you pamper him, your horse relaxes. He loves it! At the same time, you get a chance to check that his whole body is in good health. The time you spend together on grooming will strengthen your bond of friendship.

QUESTION

☆ When is it time for a shower?

Only when it's hot: no one likes to shower in the cold! Make sure the water isn't too cool and be careful not to let it splash in his eyes, ears, or nose.

SOFT BRUSH

3 Smooth the hair with a soft brush

4 And make it shine with a damp cloth!

DAMP CLOTH

5 Last step: Wipe his eyes and nostrils with a damp sponge.

SPONGE

✪ Now on to his hooves!

Earth and stones can collect under his feet and must be removed.

THE HOOF PICK

AN AREA TO AVOID!

AREA TO CLEAN

✪ Often, a farrier will clean a horse's hooves, but you may be able to learn how to do this too.

✪ The crowning touch

▶ **His mane**
Comb it often to avoid knots.

▶ **His tail**
Use a soft brush to clean the dirt and brush out any knots.

CAREFUL! SOME PARTS ARE VERY SENSITIVE.

FEED ME!

HORSES ARE STURDY ANIMALS, BUT THEY DO HAVE DELICATE STOMACHS. TO KEEP A HORSE IN GOOD HEALTH, YOU MUST FEED HIM THE RIGHT STUFF!

The menu

⭐ GRAZING IN THE GRASS

A variety of high quality grasses is the best food source for horses. Bluegrass, bromegrass, or wheatgrass, mixed with alfalfa or clover, make the perfect meal.

⭐ FILL ME UP!

During the winter season, there is no grass available for grazing. Horses must fill up on hay and straw instead.

⭐ A LITTLE "DESSERT"

Horses love carrots — and carrots are full of vitamins! Other favorite treats include apples cut into quarters, hard bread, and sugar cubes. Remember it is dessert — so don't overdo it!

⭐ SOMETHING EXTRA

Grain like oats, barley, and corn are a good source of added nutrition. The amount needed depends on a horse's breed, age, and activity level.

⭐ BIG EATER, LITTLE STOMACH

Horses have small stomachs, so they need to graze for several hours a day. This way they can take in small amounts of food at a time that can be slowly digested.

⭐ I'm thirsty!

A horse can drink up to 13 gallons of water each day. They must have access to clean water at all times.

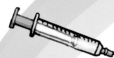

⭐ Hello, Doctor?

A horse cannot tell his owner if he is not feeling well. That's why it's so important to watch for any sign of injury or discomfort. An annual checkup by a veterinarian can prevent small problems from turning into big ones.

Coughing: the horse may have caught a virus, or might be allergic to mold or mildew in the straw or the hay.

A dull coat that is flaky: he might have fleas or an allergy from insect bites.

He scratches, rolls, looks at his flanks: he may have a stomach ache. These cramps might become very serious. This is an emergency!

VERMIFUGE

⭐ REMINDER

Don't feed a horse just before or after a workout.

Don't let him drink immediately after strenuous exercise.

PORTRAIT

⭐ THE HORSE DENTIST

A horse's teeth continue to grow for most of his life and are naturally ground down in the process of eating. Sometimes they grind down at different rates and become irregular in length, making it difficult to eat properly. That's when it's time to call the horse dentist!

⭐ 💗 A HEARTY HORSE 💗

THE AKHAL-TEKE

This breed is a legendary horse if there ever was one! The akhal-teke has been raised in the steppes of Asia for 2500 years, and has a coat of metallic reflections that is truly unique! Plus, this horse's endurance is really amazing.

HORSE WHISPERING

LONG AGO, BRUTE FORCE WAS OFTEN USED TO TRAIN HORSES. OUCH! TODAY, A GENTLER, MORE RESPECTFUL TECHNIQUE IS PREFERRED. TRAINERS WHO USE THIS TECHNIQUE ARE OFTEN REFERRED TO AS "HORSE WHISPERERS."

✪ MONTY ROBERTS

At the age of 13, Monty Roberts took off alone into the Nevada desert to study wild Mustangs. He observed a non-verbal communication between the horses which he incorporated into a nonviolent training approach called "Join-Up".

✪ A quiet revolution

Horrified by the violence used during the training of horses, some cowboys began devising new training methods. Many were inspired by the "gentling" techniques often used by Native Americans.

✪ PAT PARELLI

Pat Parelli's method, "Natural Horsemanship", is based on mutual respect. The rider listens to his horse, and the horse listens to his rider! The method proposes seven games that will help horse and rider learn to communicate with each other.

✪ AT ONE WITH THE HORSE

Horse whispering is based on observing and working to understand the natural behavior of horses. Even when it is tame, a horse will always keep its wild nature. So how does it live in the wild?

✪ THE RULES OF THE HERD

Horses live in herds made up of a male (stallion), plus many females (mares) and their young. The stallion is in charge. Some mares are more dominant than others, depending on age, strength and personality.

HISTORY

JAMES SULLIVAN MAY HAVE BEEN THE ORIGINAL "HORSE WHISPERER". WAY BACK IN THE EARLY 1800'S, HE WOULD LOCK HIMSELF IN A STALL WITH A WILD HORSE AND WITHIN SEVERAL HOURS, TAME THE ANIMAL. HOW DID HE DO IT? IT'S STILL A MYSTERY . . .

⭐ Tips for training

☀ Try something different— break your routine. This will make a horse more attentive and strengthen your relationship with each other.

☀ If a horse is fearful in certain situations, organize short but frequent training sessions to help him overcome his fears.

☀ Be consistent. Don't confuse a horse by constantly changing the rules or expectations.

☀ Spend lots of time with horses —that's how you really get to know them . . .

☀ Read books about horses and learn how they "think."

⭐ MARTHE KILEY-WORTHINGTON

This English specialist in animal communication lobbied for the respect of a horse's natural rhythm of life. On her farm, horses lived in family groups. Young foals were not separated from their mothers. Instead, they followed beside her as she worked.

⭐ LEARNING FROM MOM

A young horse finds his place in the world by imitating his elders and learning to respect them!

SADDLE UP!

⭐ LET'S LEARN HOW TO BRIDLE AND SADDLE A HORSE!

⭐ Bridle your horse

Working from the horse's left side, unbuckle his halter and re-buckle it around his neck: this way your horse stays tied up. Place the bridle reins onto the neck.

1

⭐ Saddle your horse

1 Working from the left side, place the front of the saddle blanket slightly in front of the horse's withers.

2 Offer the bit to your horse. If he won't open his mouth, press your thumb into the corner of his lips. Don't worry—he has no teeth in this area!

3 Place the crown piece over one ear, then over the other (gently!) and pull out his forelock towards the front.

3 Walk around to the right side of the horse and bring down the girth. Return to his left side and bring the girth up around his stomach. Buckle the strap under the saddle.

2 Drape the girth (the strap that goes around the horse's belly) over the saddle then place the saddle onto the blanket. The "swell" of the saddle should rest neatly over the horse's withers.

⭐ ADJUST THE THROAT LATCH: YOU SHOULD BE ABLE TO FIT YOUR FIST IN BETWEEN STRAP AND HORSE.

4 Attach the nose-band.

5 Buckle up the throat latch.

THE WELL DRESSED RIDER

⭐ Wearing a riding helmet is a must. The rest of your outfit is really up to you. You can start by digging through your closet!

⭐ What's important is comfort and safety

⭐ A good RIDING HAT is often a solid shell covered in black velvet.

⭐ Some HELMETS have a large visor to better protect you from the sun and rain.

⭐ ENGLISH RIDING PANTS are stretchy and reinforced inside at the knees.

⭐ FRIENDLY ADVICE
It's fine to wear your favorite pants, but you might want to avoid jeans with heavy stitching that can cause irritations...

⭐ HOW DO I GET STARTED?
For a trial lesson, most riding schools will lend you what you need. If you decide to continue, you will need a basic helmet and boots. As you advance in your skills, you may have to replace these—but there's no need to buy the fancy stuff right away!

⭐ HALF CHAPS are worn with paddock BOOTS to support and protect your calves from chafing.

⭐ IT'S UP TO YOU TO CHOOSE A NICE TOP!

★ KEEP YOUR HAIR OUT OF YOUR EYES!

As a matter of safety, girls are asked to tie their hair back.

✹ **Classic: triple braid.** Make three braids with your hair, then braid the braids together.

✹ **Modern: Speedy coils.** Separate your hair into two low ponytails. Roll up each ponytail and secure with a rubber band.

★ Classic Outfit

Someday you may want to be in an English riding competition. When you do, you will probably need this complete outfit: Top: a blue or black blazer, a white shirt, gloves. Bottom: light tan riding pants, boots.

EXPERT ADVICE

★ How to choose your riding helmet

✹ Your helmet must be labeled ASTM/SEI-certified.

✹ To make sure you have the right fit, try on your helmet without buckling it and move your head in all directions. Does it stay in place? Then it's perfect!

★ NO TWO ARE ALIKE

Here are some ideas on how to decorate your riding hat!

✹ **Country** Cut out flowers from wallpaper and glue them onto your hat.

COUNTRY

✹ **Autograph** Write your first name with special fabric paint.

Lilou

AUTOGRAPH

✹ **Ribbons** Create patterns out of colorful ribbons.

RIBBONS →

CLIMB ABOARD!

⭐ NOW YOU KNOW HOW TO GROOM A HORSE, HOW TO SADDLE AND BRIDLE, AND EVEN WHAT KIND OF CLOTHES TO WEAR WHEN YOU RIDE. THE NEXT STEP IS TO MOUNT UP!

⭐ TO ADJUST THE STIRRUP TO THE CORRECT LENGTH, THE STIRRUP LEATHER SHOULD BE ABOUT THE SAME LENGTH AS YOUR ARM.

TRICKS AND TIPS

⭐ Easy does it!

Be gentle with your horse: move lightly and take care not to hurt his back.

1 With your left hand, hold the reins tightly and grab onto his mane.

2 Place your left foot one third of the way into the stirrup.

3 Grab the cantle (the raised portion on the back of the saddle) with your right hand and push off with your right leg.

⭐ CHECK AND DOUBLE CHECK!

Some horses will inflate their stomachs when you tighten the girth on a saddle. Always double check the girth before mounting— or you run the risk of having the saddle turn upside down on you!

4 Up you go! Swing your right leg over the rump of your mount... swing it high, so you don't touch it!

5 Ta-da! There you are in the saddle!

⭐ I want to come down!

No problem...

1 Put your reins in your left hand and take your feet out of the stirrups.

2 Lean towards the front and swing your right leg over the rump — (careful not to touch it!)

3 Let yourself slide down... and land lightly, on the tip of your toes, with your knees bent.

⭐ 💗💗 MY LITTLE PONY 💗💗

THE SHETLAND

This little guy is the best friend of beginning riders! He's very small, but super solid. In the Shetland Islands (north of England), the weather is bad and it's always windy. The vegetation is so sparse that sometimes he even has to eat algae!

THE WALK

You have to learn to walk before you can run! Start off slowly, learning to guide your horse the correct way.

EYES AHEAD

CHEST UP

ELBOWS NEXT TO YOUR BODY

REINS FIRM, BUT LOOSE

LEGS DROPPED

BALLS OF THE FEET ON THE STIRRUP, HEELS LOWER THAN THE TOES.

✪ Have a seat!

Having a "good seat" means being able to stay solidly in your saddle at all times. To do this, you must hold yourself correctly and attain good balance. The more you practice, the more at ease you will be!

✪ GUIDING THE HORSE

★ You can tell your horse to move forward by tightening your legs on its flanks. Do it again to make him go faster.

★ Your hands tell him which direction to go in and when to stop.

★ The weight of your body also helps you give him instructions. Look in the direction you want to turn and your body weight will naturally shift. This helps the horse sense which way you want to go.

★ Don't forget to use your voice! Use a voice when you are pleased with him, a firmer voice when you need to get his attention!

✪ WOBBLY-BOBBLY

The first time you ride a horse, you'll probably feel a little unsteady. That's normal: when a horse walks, the rolling movement of his spine and the swaying of his neck are very pronounced. Just try to relax and go with it!

✪ 1-2-3-4, 1-2-3-4 . . .

When walking, the horse places each foot down in the same way: right back leg, right front leg, left back leg, left front leg, and so on . . .

RIGHT BACK LEG

⭐ A Rider in Action

⭐ SPEEDING UP

☀ To go faster, tighten your calves and lean forward slightly.

⭐ WHOA! STOP!

☀ Lean back when you want to stop.

☀ Tighten the reins slightly by lifting your wrists.

⭐ TURNING

☀ There are several ways to tell your horse to turn. The simplest is by "opening the reins." Hold out the hand on the side where you want to turn, keeping your elbow close to your body.

☀ Move your other hand forward slightly at the same time.

☀ Exert slight leg pressure so the horse doesn't slow down while turning.

☀ Turn your own chest slightly while looking in the direction you want to turn.

⭐ A LIGHT HAND

Hold the reins lightly and never pull hard on them. You could hurt the horse's mouth!

RIGHT FRONT LEG

LEFT BACK LEG

LEFT FRONT LEG

CRUISING SPEED: 4 MILES PER HOUR

THE TROT

PRACTICAL ADVICE

THIS GAIT IS VERY USEFUL AT RIDING SCHOOL OR WHEN YOU GO FOR A STROLL— BUT IT CAN BE A LITTLE UNCOMFORTABLE UNTIL YOU LEARN HOW TO DO IT RIGHT!

✪ FROM WALKING TO TROTTING

To ask your horse to move into a trot, adjust your reins, kick your legs and release your reins a little so that he can move forward.

✪ Posting

One way to make trotting more comfortable is to "post." Lean your upper body slightly forward, lifting yourself up out of your saddle with the first beat, and sit back down on the second... and then start again! You might want to train yourself first on a horse that is standing still.

✪ ONCE YOU HAVE MASTERED POSTING, YOU WILL FIND IT VERY COMFORTABLE. THE SAME THING GOES FOR YOUR MOUNT: WHEN YOU LIFT YOURSELF UP, YOU ARE RESTING HIS BACK!

✪ SIT DOWN,   STAND UP,   SIT DOWN...

✪ CAREFUL NOW!

* ☀ Keep your back straight.
* ☀ Lift yourself up and sit back down lightly.

✪ IN THE WILD

In nature, the horse walks slowly. He may trot for long trips - and he only canters or gallops when he is fleeing danger.

✪ CLIP CLOP, CLIP CLOP...

When he is trotting, the horse lifts and puts down one diagonal (front leg and opposite hind leg) after another. Left diagonal (front left leg and hind right leg)

DIAGONAL LEFT (FRONT LEFT LEG AND HIND RIGHT LEG)

SUSPENSION

⭐ The sitting trot

Different from posting—the goal is to keep your backside glued to your saddle without bouncing! Relax your pelvis so that it can absorb the maximum movements of the horse.

⭐ CAREFUL NOW!

☀ Keep your chest facing forward.

☀ Stay relaxed: don't pull on the reins, and don't push on the stirrups.

⭐ TROTTING RACES

The principle is the same as any other horse race—only here the horse must cover the distance by trotting. If he breaks the trot, he is disqualified!

CHECK THIS OUT!

⭐ ♥♥ FIVE GAIT PONY ♥♥

THE ICELANDIC PONY

Incredible! They call him the "five speed horse". His gaits include the walk, trot, canter, tolt, and the flying pace! The flying pace is when the horse moves two legs from the same side at the same time (front right leg and back right leg – then front left leg and back left leg.)

Tolting is like walking, but much faster, with the legs being lifted very high.

DIAGONAL RIGHT (FRONT RIGHT LEG AND HIND LEFT LEG)

SUSPENSION

CRUISING SPEED: 9 MILES PER HOUR

THE CANTER

RACING DOWN THE LANE, FULL SPEED . . .
FANTASTIC! BUT ALSO KIND OF SCARY.
DON'T WORRY: ONCE YOU KNOW WHAT
YOU'RE DOING, YOU'RE
GOING TO LOVE IT!

★ And we're off!

Keep your shoulders slightly towards the back, your head high, and your legs circling the horse's flanks. Now follow the "see-saw" movements of his gait with your pelvis, and keep your hands in rhythm with his neck movements . . . Easy and really fun!

GOING FROM A TROT TO A CANTER

✹ Speed up your trot by pressing the horse's flanks several times with your calves. Unbalanced, he will "fall" into a canter.

ADVICE FROM LILY

★ WHAT NOT TO DO

Don't tense your legs

Don't pull on the reins: you might hurt the horse. Also, he will defend himself by shaking his head . . . and that could cause you to take a tumble!

★ 1, 2, 3, INTO THE AIR . . .

The canter is a three-beat gait, plus one beat of suspension.

IF HE CANTERS TO THE RIGHT, THE HORSE PUTS DOWN | HIS HIND LEFT LEG | HIS FRONT LEFT LEG AND BACK RIGHT LEG TOGETHER | HIS FRONT RIGHT LEG

✪ Full speed ahead!

The faster you go, the more you shake! To better absorb the shock, lean forwards a little bit while cantering. You will also relieve the pressure on your horse's back!

✪ The jockey's position

A jockey keeps the stirrups very short and leans far forward to encourage the horse to go faster. It's not really very comfortable . . .

✪ THE FASTEST HORSE

During a 1945 race in Mexico, Big Racket ran almost 44 miles an hour. That speed has not been equaled to this day!

RECORD!

SUSPENSION

IF THE HORSE CANTERS TO THE LEFT, HE PUTS DOWN:

HIS HIND RIGHT LEG

HIS FRONT RIGHT LEG AND HIND LEFT LEG TOGETHER

HIS FRONT LEFT LEG

FOLLOWED BY THE TIME OF SUSPENSION

AROUND THE WORLD WITH HORSES

Once upon a time, living and working with horses was very common. What was once so ordinary is much less common today. Yet, all over the world, people are still riding and carrying on ancient traditions...

★ GAUCHOS (GOU′ CHŌZ) OF ARGENTINA

The grassy plains of the pampas are filled with cattle ranches where thousands of gauchos continue to herd cattle. Their horses, criollos (krē ō′ lōz), are intelligent and sturdy—and can sometimes live up to 40 years!

★ THE COWBOYS

To manage the herd, the large ranches of the Western United States now use 4x4 vehicles and even small planes. But cowboys still depend on their quarter horses, with their amazing agility and speed, to help capture an animal or rescue a calf that is stranded in the depths of a canyon.

THE GUARDIANS OF CAMARGUE (KA MARG')

The Guardians are similar to American cowboys. They are responsible for rounding up the wild black bulls that graze on the land in southeastern France. The Camargue horses they ride are muscular and sure-footed.

YABUSAME ARCHERS OF JAPAN

The art of yabusame - archery on horseback - has been practiced in Japan for over 15 centuries. Today, this art is still a part of sacred ceremonies, where the horseback riders invoke the gods to attract peace and prosperity to their country.

THE AUSTRALIAN STOCKMEN

When the Australians replaced their horses with cars, they released many of their horses back into nature. Today, these wild horses, called "brumbies", number about 600,000. Stockmen (Australian cowboys) sometimes round up and capture a few of these horses to showcase in rodeos.

THE ARAB RIDERS

The Arabian horse is one of the most popular breeds in the world. And for good reason! They are beautiful, fast, and have amazing stamina cultivated from working in their harsh desert environment over the last 1,000 years!

JUST FOR FUN!

★ YOU LOVE HORSES. AND SO DO YOUR FRIENDS! WHY NOT MAKE THEM SMALL GIFTS WITH A HORSE THEME FOR A GALLOPING GOOD TIME!

★ PAPER CHAIN SURPRISE

1• Cut out a long strip of paper measuring 11 by 5 inches.

2• Fold it as illustrated in the drawing.

3• Draw a horse by following the model and cut. But be careful! The paper chain will be held by the folded sides, so do not cut too much!

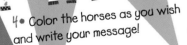

4• Color the horses as you wish and write your message!

★ ANCHOR THE HEAD ONTO A WOODEN BASE WITH A METAL ROD.

★ HORSE HEAD STATUE

1• Carve a horse's head out of modeling clay.

2• Cover it with strips of wet papier mache. For smaller areas, you can use tissue paper.

3• When it is really dry, paint it to look like your favorite horse

★ WINDOW CARD

1• Choose a pretty horse picture.

2• Cut out a card from stiff paper. Fold the card in half. Glue the photo onto the inside.

3• Cut out a window on the front of the card, allowing part of the picture inside to show.

TA-DA! A HORSE LOVER'S CARD!

Riding high into the New Year! Love, Lily

WRITE A SHORT NOTE.

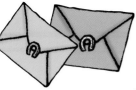

★ HORSE ENVELOPE

1• Carefully unglue an envelope, to use as a model.

2• Find a pretty page in a horse magazine. Cut it into the size and shape of your model envelope. Try to choose the right framing!

3• Now fold up and glue your envelope.

ADVICE FROM LILY

★ BOOK MARK

1• Trace out the model shown, or get inspired by a horse you like and draw your own!

2• Make your bookmark out of heavyweight paper.

3• Decorate both sides of the bookmark.

LOOK: IT KEEPS YOUR PAGE WITH ITS LEG SO YOU DON'T LOSE IT!

★ HORSES LIKE PRESENTS TOO!

What kind of gift would a horse enjoy?

★ A treat: a few cubes of sugar, some apples, some carrots or a nice bunch of beets!

★ An outing: does he spend winter in a stable? Grant him a day of freedom, by letting him have mini-vacations out in the fields.

★ A cuddle: a nice grooming session or a massage . . .

YOU ARE THE ARTIST!

WOULD YOU LIKE TO DRAW YOUR FAVORITE ANIMAL? HERE ARE A FEW IDEAS TO INSPIRE YOU . . .

★ A little sketch

This horse made from lines and squares is very easy to draw—and to animate! Have fun creating different moods and adventures . . .

★ Almost real

Follow the steps to draw this picture of a horse. Sketch the simple shapes to help with proportion and weight—then gradually fill in to complete your drawing.

4 NOW ALL THAT'S LEFT IS TO COLOR IT IN WITH THE MARKINGS OF YOUR FAVORITE HORSE!

3 FINISH WITH THE LEGS. THESE ARE TRICKY . . . PRESS LIGHTLY WITH YOUR PENCIL, SO THAT YOU CAN ERASE YOUR MARKS!

2 THEN DRAW TWO LARGE CIRCLES FOR THE BODY

1 START WITH THE HEAD . . .

✪ Prehistoric

 1 Blow up the stylized horse stencil. Make several photocopies until you get the size that you like.

DRAWING MADE WITH A STENCIL

STENCIL

2 Trace the stencil, and put it onto a light piece of cardboard. Hollow out the shape (ask a grown-up for help). Place the stencil on a large piece of paper and paint using colors inspired from your original.

✪ THE TARPAN HORSE

With its rough mane and coat, and a small, high-backed body, it looks like the cave horses that used to be all over prehistoric Europe. But in the 19th century, the last of those horses were captured in Poland and the race disappeared ... So who is this in the photo? This is a "new" tarpan: recreated by breeding other horses that most resembled it!

✪ The Original

Discovered in 1944, the Lascaux Cave in France has some of the most beautiful examples of prehistoric art on its walls. These paintings date back about 15,000 years. There are 355 horses drawn on the walls!

LEGENDS AND GHOST STORIES

⭐ THEY FLY THROUGH THE AIR, TRANSFORM THEMSELVES AT WILL, AND BRING THEIR HEROES TO VICTORY... HORSES ARE ALSO SUPER-HEROES!

⭐ Amazon horseback riders

Greek legends are full of Amazons. These ruthless female warriors always battled on horseback. Their particular riding style, used only by women, has endured even today: it's sometimes called "Amazon style".

⭐ LUCKY CHARM

If you find a horse-shoe with it's open end pointing towards you, it means good luck! Nail it onto your door – facing up – so that the good luck won't fall out ... Do you believe it?

Leonardo's Dream

Imagine a white horse with a long, twisted horn . . . In the Middle Ages and during the Renaissance, the beautiful unicorn symbolized purity. Was it really too wild to tame? Not completely! Leonardo de Vinci describes how to handle it: "As soon as it sees an innocent young girl, the unicorn approaches her and falls asleep at her feet . . ."

DIVINE STABLES

✹ Pegasus

The story goes that a Greek prince tried to rise up to the kingdom of the gods by riding this winged horse. He was thrown off, and only Pegasus reached Olympia.

PEGASUS

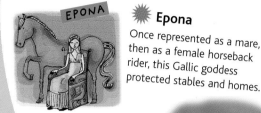

EPONA

✹ Epona

Once represented as a mare, then as a female horseback rider, this Gallic goddess protected stables and homes.

✹ Sleipnir (slāp'-nir)

The Nordic god Odin rode this horse (with eight legs!) on earth, over the oceans and in the air.

SLEIPNIR

Giant mysteries

England counts more than fifty giant figures that were created in chalk. 17 of these are horses. The white Westbury horse from the southern part of the country dates from the 9th century. Like the 16 others, nobody knows its true significance.

⭐ SCARY STUFF

✹ Evil spirit

In Scotland, rivers and lakes are haunted by Kelpie, a pony that appears at night to lost travelers. Bad luck awaits anyone who tries to ride him; they end up drowning.

✹ Bad omen

A sick person who dreams of a black horse will soon leave for the after-life . . . that's what people in the Middle-Ages believed!

SOME VOCABULARY WORDS FOR THE HORSE LOVER

HERE ARE SOME DEFINITIONS ABOUT HORSES AND THEIR ENVIRONMENT.

B

Bar: an interdental space situated between the horse's incisor and molar teeth; this is where the bit is placed.

Bare Patch: a piece of skin without pigment or hair, situated at the tip of a horse's nose or lips.

Bedding: a bed of straw (sawdust, wood chips...) that is spread onto the ground of the stable to insulate it from the cold and from urine.

Bit: a piece of metal placed inside a horse's mouth. Linked to the reins, it allows the rider to guide his horse.

Boxing: kicking with its front legs.

Bridle: harness which is placed over the horse's head so that we can guide him.

Brood Mare: Mare destined for reproduction.

Bucking: kicking with its hind legs.

C

Cantle: the raised portion on the back of the saddle

Chaps: abbreviation of the Spanish word chaparajos. Leg covers that the rider wears over his pants to protect them from rubbing.

Coat: the color of fur and mane of a horse.

Colt: Male horse up to 4 years old

Curry comb: brush with teeth or short nails used to remove large bits of dirt from a horse's coat.

D

Dorsal stripe: colored stripe running down the back of a horse—from the mane into the tail

E

Ethology: the science of studying animal behavior. Training by "horse whisperers" is based on ethology.

F

Farrier: A professional trained to care for a horse's hooves.

Fetlock: tufts of hair situated behind the horse's ankle. Some are longer than others, and they protect the most sensitive parts of the horse's foot from humidity, mud...

First Training: First training of a young horse, whose objective is to get him to accept the saddle, the bit and a rider.

Foal: name given to a newborn horse from the time it is born until January 1st of the following year.

Founder: a disease of the horse's foot, due to food that is too rich, or due to a lack of exercise.

G

Gait: a horse's way of moving. There are three main gaits: walking, trotting and cantering.

Groom: a person who takes care of racehorses.

Grooming: cleaning the horse, with the help of a selection of brushes.

H

Halter: a head harness. When a lead line is attached, it allows for walking and tying up a horse.

Hand: unit used to measure a horse. 1 hand = 4 inches

Hindquarters: the back part of a horse, comprised of the croup, the tail and the hind limbs.

Hippology: the study of horses.

I

Indoor arena: covered space where equestrian sports are practiced.

L

Lead Rope: a cord linked to the halter, used to hold, lead and tie up a horse.

M

Mane: the long stiff hair growing on the back of or around the neck of a horse.

Mare: a female horse over 4 years of age

Mash: a light and nutritious meal fed to horses with digestive problems.

P

Paddock: holding area where a horse is kept untied. It is also a designated area for horses to be shown before a race or competition.

Pick the hooves: Clean the horse's hooves.

R

Reins: long lanyards, most often made out of leather. Linked to the bit, they serve to direct the horse.

Riding Bareback: riding without a saddle.

Rubdown: vigorously scrubbing the horse with a straw brush or another kind of brush.

S

Saddle Blanket: cloth placed between the saddle and the horse's back to absorb sweat and reduce friction.

Seat: A rider's ability to keep his balance under any circumstance. A rider has a good or bad seat, according to whether he holds himself well or badly.

Stable: an enclosed, individual stall where the horse is left untied.

Splash: a white spot on a horse's leg.

Stable Hand: a person in charge of the care and well-being of the horses in a stable.

Stallion: male horse reserved for breeding.

Stud Book: a genealogical registry in which all officially recognized horses of a breed are registered and therefore "have papers".

Sweat Scraper: a dull blade that won't cut, used to clear the sweat off a horse after a workout or to clear off the water after a shower. Originally made of metal, today they can be found made out of plastic or rubber.

V

Vices: a bad habit that a horse sometimes develops due to boredom.

W

Washed: when the mane is lighter than the coat of a horse.

Wither: a prominent part of the horse, situated at the base of the neck.

Workout: training a horse.

Y

Yearling: Name given to designate a young horse between one and two years old. Term usually used referring to thoroughbred horses. .

**If you liked *The Horse Lover's Book*, here is another
We Both Read® Book you are sure to enjoy!**

The race is on! It's the annual swim competition and it looks like the boy's team is going to lose to the girl's team again! The boys think some girls stole their mascot, named Lucky. Without their mascot, the boys are convinced they will never win. Now, it's up to Sam and his friends to solve the mystery. If they can find Lucky, maybe they can also solve the old mystery of Pirate's Point!